BOS
01/09
5/15 wuc

D1513798

Get **more** out of libraries

Please return or renew this item by the last date shown.

You can renew online at www.hants.gov.uk/library

Or by phoning 0845 603 5631

Hampshire
County Council

C014441508

ALSO BY GRETA STODDART

At Home in the Dark
2001

GRETA STODDART
Salvation Jane

ANVIL PRESS POETRY

Published in 2008
by Anvil Press Poetry Ltd
Neptune House 70 Royal Hill London SE10 8RF

Copyright © Greta Stoddart 2008

ISBN 978 0 85646 411 9

This book is published
with financial assistance from
Arts Council England

A catalogue record for this book
is available from the British Library

The moral rights of the author have been asserted in
accordance with the Copyright, Designs and Patents Act 1988

Designed and set in Monotype Bell by Anvil
Printed and bound in Great Britain
by Hobbs the Printers Ltd

Hampshire County Library	
C014441508	
Askews	Jan-2009
821.92	£7.95
	9780856464119

Contents

ACKNOWLEDGEMENTS

Acknowledgements are due to the editors of the following publications in which (versions of) these poems first appeared:

Magma, Metre, New Welsh Review, New Writing 14 (*Granta* and The British Council), *Poetry London, Poetry Review, The Spectator* and the *TLS*.

Thanks to Alice Oswald, Peter Oswald, Shakespeare's Globe & The Wordsworth Trust for commissioning and publishing 'On Pont Royal' in the anthology *Earth has not any thing to shew more fair* and to Lavinia Greenlaw, The Royal Society of Medicine and Calouste Gulbenkian Foundation for commissioning and publishing 'Want' in *Signs and Humours*: The Poetry of Medicine.

And to Arts Council England, London for a grant in 2004 which helped towards the writing of this book.

Salvation Jane

Pupil

I could no more know
myself than this flame
seated in the air
one quarter of an inch
above its burnt root
– so self-contained a form
you'd think it held in ice –

no more know that flame
than one drop of rain
or a single leaf
let alone this draught
slicing in across the sill
nudging the little
corpse-boat of a fly;

no more know you, fly,
than this cat – the cat
perhaps but what about
the way it holds us
in a gaze so void
of an idea of self
our own can only fail.

Were we to return
that look we might learn
to take something from
nothing, might begin
to steady and see,
figure who we are
in that slit black flame.

Instrument

All this wind and rain could so easily go
without saying (and it does, we know it does)

as could, as ever, birds – no, swifts! fluid,
workmanlike, fixing rips in the sky.

Here we go again, saying stuff,
coming up against this great easy other.

To what good isn't clear but who's to stop us tonight
as we make our beery diesel public transport way home

calling up a bird (never mind the name),
a small bursting thing – I have him

in a clearing, the world at his feet,
his chest giving in and out like a pedal.

A Puzzle in Four Seasons

Look at us. It must be Christmas.
Our heads are bowed, the lamp close.
We could be cracking a code
or a body, so intent are we tonight

on *Spring* whose large foreground
of wild daffodils could take us all winter.
We check the lid from time to time like artists
more absorbed in what they're doing than what's there:

a village coming into itself
all at once, in all weathers;
yielding itself to nothing more
than the hours of its own slow resurrection.

It's not often we come together like this.
Nor do we believe for one minute
in this village or its charmed stoicism.
We attend to it quietly, with quick fingers.

Salvation Jane

What is Salvation Jane?

Little purple sturdy thistle,
dicot weed of the Boraginaceae

'But it's beekeepers' gold,
     a sun-chopped sea of violet trumpetheads
          – a god's bright nodding flock!'

And Paterson's Curse?

Little purple sturdy thistle,
dicot weed of the Boraginaceae

'But it's a noxious rough hairy-leaved herb,
     a chemical-resistant infestor of cereals;
          it chokes pastures, poisons cattle.'

Who gives these names, who tends them?

Men and women who look up at the dark
     gold-tinted clouds and mouth 'Heaven',
          who run for their lives shouting 'Storm!'

Faithful

In dreams it comes to us to walk on water
and fly over glowing towns but when we wake
our shoulders ache and the casual flair
with which we overcame ourselves is gone.

Though some awake or in a waking dream
can stare at the sun till it turns black,
ease back on a bed of broken glass
or, like the fakir, stroll out of one fire

and into another. It's still a mystery
to me that time I woke, my ankles flecked,
the dull bloom of a bruise, when all I recalled
of the night before was a good soak, a book.

As is this. Me, here, content
night after night to bed down with you
but turn to the window we keep shut fast –
the better to make a running jump, the break.

Want

the voice of an unconceived child

The more you look the more remote
I am to you not as a star but a stone

kicked to the edge of a lane two roads in
from the sea in a dead-end town.

You won't think to look there
because you're here

in this bright room, bent over the blur
of threads that's led you here where

you daren't move for fear of upsetting
whatever it is that's stopping you getting

what you want – a tower
of fine bone china

in a dark corner,
growing higher and higher;

here where you come closest to me,
me who is really you – you

as small, knuckled want,
impotent, clean, clock-watching want.

But you know how it is.
I'll come to you when you're a mess,

pissed probably, putting it about,
when you've loosed yourself from the thought

of yourself and world crashes in with its crowds
of stricken infants, its mad array of flowers.

O oestrogen, astrology, buseralin and cells,
HCG, Day 14, the transmigration of souls!

It's all more than you could ever know.
So stop, little no-mother, come and throw

yourself back onto a strong wind –
take in the sky, hold on to nothing.

The Wait

Two hundred and seventy seven days
I ticked off and had I had an hour-glass
might've watched each minute down to the last
drop of grain, then turned it over again,

for you took your time, clocking up
fat, cartilage, bone – son, or daughter,
in taking form you summoned from me water,
milk, an extra forty cups of blood.

But what you took was for me a given,
a trade-off – my weeks for your pounds;
what I did and what you were grounds
for a perfectly balanced, a good argument.

As they tugged you out I had this thought:
how much sand, how many bags of sugar?
As it was, I watched the needle quiver
at what you were then plunge back down to nought.

You drew breath

as a boy draws something silver from a river,
an angler from the sea a bale of weed;
as a woman draws herself from a bath,
as blood is drawn from a vein.
You drew breath as thread is drawn through
the eye of a needle, wet sheets through a mangle,
as steel is drawn through a die to make wire
and oil draws up through wick its flag of fire.
You drew breath as a reservoir draws from a well
of ink and a mouth and a nose and eyes are drawn,
as a sheet is drawn from under the dying
and over the heads of the dead.
You drew breath as the last wheezing pint is drawn,
as money and a bow and the tide are drawn;
as up over her head a woman draws
a dress and down onto her a man.
You drew breath as a cloud draws its pall
across the moon, across the car park
where a sky-blue line draws the way
all the way to Maternity; as all in blue
they drew a semi-circle round the bed,
a line and then a knife across the skin;
as in another room someone drew
a curtain round its runner, a hand across
a pair of finished eyes. You drew breath
as they drew you – besmeared and blue – out
and sublime was your fury at being drawn
into this air, this theatre; you drew breath
for the first time – for a second I held mine.

At Play

There's a cow
deep in the lavender bush, the remote
is in a shoe and who

put the digger
in the knicker drawer, the farmer
in the loo? Some creature's

been and re-
arranged our small plot according
to some inscrutable law

of its own.
The path is strewn with raisins and bricks,
there's a bear on his back in the oven.

A one-eyed duck
sits for days on *Hard Times*
and a sailor's face-down in the mud.

See how
each scene is made to come about
with the questionable air

of things stopped
rather than ended, for this little maker
grows cold to what

is done with,
    moves on without so much as a
        All to the good, you wreaker

            /creator of havoc
                wise to not mind meaning
       for now, for this, you bundle

      of nerves and decision
   is your first grasp of things. That hole
        you dug for the broken man.

The Street Lamp

Maybe it's this orange light
that has me up
in the middle of the night
when sleep ought to have
taken hold and placed us
god knows where
with whom and how and why

or was that the baby's cry
turning into something else
and rising that has me rising
not to him but to look
down at the street and see
in a pool of light – what *is* that –
a stain, his small coat?

Body seems to know
but mind, sleep-filled
and slow with notions,
ups and follows
(whatever it is it has that
self-possessed and desolate look
of a thing left behind);

and heart that knows
starts to knock and will not
take comfort from the street lamp
who stands over our house
like a guardian angel,
head inclined but with no arms
or wings to gather whosoever in.

Even Here

Even here, this Peckham I'm in:
these spacey treks pushing
baby round the Rye in the rain;

the screech of parakeets
lime-quick among the London planes,
the still, gloopy lake;

all this Victoriana, this long kitchen
with its slugtrails and foxstink,
this garden pinned under a flight path

I'll come to miss
or make of it
something it wasn't.

Just as yesterday I stepped off
the train in that place
I've set my heart on

– that salt hit,
a seagull's old *yearning yearning*,
its scrappy wheeling flight –

and stood there knowing the time
would come when I'd long for it,
be gone from it, and long for it.

In the Kitchen

I'm reading and reading this line
about the horse 'living outside of time'.
Surely not. Surely the horse is deep in,
up to his neck in time.

Horse now is horse then.
Horse always with his big teeth,
his wide saddle-warm back,
the swivel and twitch of his ears;

horse felled to one side,
the thick flick of his tail;
the calm and the startle
in his deep brown eyes.

All this without him knowing
which is like time not knowing
what it is, or knowing only
what it is as it happens

in the silence of the kitchen;
the clock in the silence of the kitchen,
the horse clipclopping past the window
open in the silence of the kitchen.

Really

What's the point of a vase
painted with pink and white roses

or a fruit bowl enamelled
with passion-fruit and pomegranates?

Isn't it enough for tulips to soar
from a plain earthenware jug,

for bananas and pears and tangerines to sit
higgledy-piggledy in a glass bowl

and be themselves
the bulging colourful heart of a room?

And the child in a photo
on the wall fixed

in light, in a smile
that won't fail, is dead

to the one who's now being dragged
kicking and screaming round the shops

by a woman whose heart has gone cold,
who says she doesn't know why she bothers.

Verfremdungseffekt

Our budget got the biggest laugh.
We blew half of it on a fat hack in a Chinese
"All You Can Eat for a Tenner!"

We sat and watched as he helped himself to thirds
of Ham Foo Yung – next day we read his piece
on a local midwife's prize ornamental cabbage.

We pulled out all the tricks: natty flip
of a baking sheet for thunder, our hero walking
away to a pair of hand-clopped brogues.

Pulled them out literally, you understand.
We'd read our Brecht and were completely sold;
no bourgeois suspension of disbelief for us!

So really the conditions couldn't've been better
that July evening in Speke Youth Club where,
impossible to get a black-out – the sun, the skylights –

we still crept on 'stage', careful not to follow
the shredded pitch-markings nor make eye contact
with the audience we outnumbered five to three

(had we an ounce of common decency
we'd've pulled the show and paid their refund
in the pub but we were young, and all that mattered).

I've forgotten every word of *Kleines Organon für das Theater*
but not how it ended that night:
our final dramatic pause filling

with the chittity-chit of swallows, the M6's rivery hum,
our faces lifting their faces up
not to some fusty old gods but a heaven

of swing ropes and gym ladders suspended there
like something unbelievable that did once and would,
with faith enough or a full house, happen again.

Plastic Bag

Snagged on a high branch
you're up there now
with shipwreck, wasteland,
a doll's limbless stare –

Look at you,
you soul of nonchalance,
you carrier of nothing
that will not die!

And though we've just seen
a film in which you starred,
waltzing feebly along a kerb,
performing your one restless thought

your true forever's fixed
wherever you happen to end up:
thornbush, gutter;

up in the attic
with your sad hoard
of baby clothes and love letters;

deep in a hole
at the end of the garden
wrapped around a house sparrow
we almost had
eating out of our hands.

The Night of the Hunter

I don't want to know
how it all began; how it marked
the beginning and the end
of the actor's directing career;
how fat he was, or sick,
what time his first Scotch.

I don't want to know
how the budget was some kind of practical joke;
how all the stars turned him down
save one old Southern Belle who hadn't worked
in years on account of the talkies
and her insufferable squawk.

I don't want to know
how the script arrived a year late,
a rambling, unfilmable tome
the size of three phone books;
how the crew were granted a share in the profits
but ended up in debt.

And please don't tell me
because I don't want to know
how that long shot of the preacher
riding silhouetted across the horizon
is really a midget on a donkey,
how it took one take;

and the spider's web glistening with dew
is nylon dipped in honey, and the stars
bulbs scatterstitched into a yard of velvet;
how it plunged like a meteorite
at the box-office.
Oh and how he hated the children.

In the *Dreams* Warehouse

Because we want to show that we are serious
about this Regal Supreme we have to pretend
that we're at home in this gloomy old depot,
that it's night and we're warm and naked, alone.
Flat on our backs in boots and coats
we've taken to this bed as to a tomb
and we the grim faithfuls long forgotten
we're here to test the Supreme's
unique honeycomb nesting system
with its two thousand six-coiled springs
and overlay of hairproof black coir ticking.

'Made up North, this one. Mill country.
All that cotton and cambric, it's in their bones.
Not a machine in sight. Weeks it takes.'
We stare up at him, his belly's overhang.
A couple of coins trickle out of your pocket.
And perhaps I've actually gone now as I find
I'm off with the Shoemaker or rather his Elves,
their sunny rags and fixed smiles,
their silent unworldly devotion to work
and you're so quiet I imagine you've found cause

to return to your obsession with the Egyptians;
the milling clusters of pyramid-builders,
their sweat-metal backs and casual deaths.
Then I see you've somehow kept one foot
flat on the ground – all this time

stalling us here in the shallows!
Come on, it's cold. Let's just decide.
Kick off – let's slide into the murky dream
of what this top-of-the-range, this ultimate-in-comfort,
this two-grand bed might make of us.

Like a Substance

As when I'm sick in bed
  and you move through it towards me
    as though through leaf-thick wood

as when that time at Heathrow
  you lifted me up through it
    as if I were eight or air

as when it used to weigh nothing
  come and go like more or less
    like come and go like wind

as when it hardens but is still
  soft like a sheet pulled between
    two people easing the task

as when we come up against it
  as to a wall of glass – pressing
    with hands and mouths our small betrayals

love, the pressure we put to bear on it

At the School Gates

I've come late
to the company of mothers,

this talk of sleep
and vaccinations,

this love they say
that'd lead them to kill.

I don't feel it
but am coming closer,

am being drawn
by a simple kinship

of hours kept:
morning bell, hometime.

I approach the gates
overcome with –

I don't know
what it is to belong

to any such group
or what to say.

Certainly not this:
that I feel like some creature

who was once driven out
because of some weakness

but who must return now
because she has young of her own

to the herd gathered here
at the edge of their territory.

Two policemen stand
in the middle of the playground.

It's dark this afternoon.
The women's breath is a kind of light;

they don't look up or make room
but something closes in around me.

Television

True, the nights were drawing in
but that wasn't only why I came
at the same early evening hour
to sit on the rug close to the fire
I couldn't be bothered to light
and face the glow of news – that week
of Hurricane Ivan: streets awash,
the woman who'd *lost everything*.

That'd be me for the evening,
phone on mute, child early to bed,
for the some small good to be had
from being told the facts behind
our increasingly stormy planet:

a tornado one calm Birmingham noon,
Boscastle half-tumbling out to sea

but then how not so long ago
hippos lumbered through the Thames

and how catastrophic the means by which
our mild grassy hills were born.

Later we are shown the stars:
how like the dead
they far and away outnumber us
who find ourselves under their
continual shining remove
but holed up, leaning in
like beggars round the one light.

Homebound

*In 1756 French writer Xavier de Maistre
undertook a nocturnal journey around his bedroom*

Cactus, etching, chipped green shade –
these things have become my intimates
on this long night-faring charade.

And though nothing does something has changed;
watching them now is like repeating a word
over and over till all it sounds is strange.

What, old things, have I become for you:
captain of a ship, perhaps, ill-equipped
but bound on a certain dogged course? It's true,

I've chosen a route through peculiar straits:
I have this blue gown, these bare feet,
a crew who by their very restraint

provide solace I never knew till now.
I'm thankful, too, for their show of constancy;
where would we be if my Nocturnus glowed,

if Lamp blackened and died? It's late. Listen.
Hollow bottle. Fl-flump of drying sails.
Lift the lid on that little house –

see the woman
with a parasol facing the wall
and stepping out in cape and boots a man?

Under the tutelage of such things I see
that even when we're still we will be moved;
that safe inside four walls we're all at sea . . .

Last night we came through a storm – such thrashing
of winds and twisting, rain-besotted gulls!
What was so wild and brainless so unhappy

is becalmed tonight. The water black.
The moon would have me climb those glittering rungs;
come day they'll be hauled in and any way back

down gone for good. I've lost the heart
for such risks, so hold by the clock's slow circle,
these four cold panes of glass.

The Move

for Maryann

It's hard to believe you'll leave this house
grief has reinforced but time stands by
for when you'll push up from that table,
move towards the door and find

you don't freeze or buckle or stall;
you're not slow-breasting through air
that holds in folds every image
you have of him released at once;

and the move isn't a heave through now
but unlocks itself without thought,
set off perhaps by a wand of light
shooting in from the door shooting

straight across the floor and up
the wall along the speckled counter
coming to naught in a fuzzy burst
on the kettle's still warm cheek;

and it is what it is – a step
back to old comforts and towards
the awkward begetting of new ones
as when you said with some rapture

Being dead is so much more alive
than dying bringing to mind the dead
whose faces seem to have arrived
at a place reached inside them.

And the move will herald an armistice
between soul – that highly-strung old thing! –
and body who gets its laissez-faire
way at last as you wipe your hands

on a tea-towel (Twenty Kinds of Leaf)
and stand at the door to look through
at the trees, noncommittal, bare,
who are alone, and salute you.

Portent

It's the sallow fields and humming grass,
It's rooks zoning into the wrong trees

It's cows lying down, a thrush's high nest,
It's how fat and tight the autumn berries

It's the zillions of things, the creeping things
And what they know and know about rain

It's what sailors see in the absence of waves:
The end of the world going on forever

It's the hard-packed snow's sudden to powder,
'Our picks useless as knives in flour'

It's the elephants lumbering up to the hills,
The acres of sand and thwack of fish

It's the tightening skull for the epileptic,
The walnut lump in the woman's breast

It's dizzy spells and pale green blisters,
It's bright red blood in the first trimester

It's this not curdling, that not mending,
It's Eve's dream, it's the earth it's the earth

It's evidence and augury,
The burning sun and the rising seas

It's us, wasted, tumbling from Heaven
Into cities of stone

The River and the Rope Bridge

Let's try and get halfway then stand firm,
rein in each rough jerk and shudder.
But the merest sway in the wind has us
wobbling hopefully on towards the bank
or crawling back to the woods we know.
The river beneath has seen it all before.
Like us it has nowhere special to go
but goes there all the same. All the same
you'd think it'd stall and darken but no,
it'd still sparkle in the sun, go on
(Go on!) if we gave up and jumped in.

On Pont Royal

*'O young woman, throw yourself into the water again so that
I may a second time have the chance of saving both of us!'*
                    THE FALL, Albert Camus

Here? No, I wouldn't. Not that I care
in reality, but there is something to be said
(and you probably said it) for doing it where –
but I'm thinking now that what you wrote I read
far too young, or is it from birth this urge
to jump and lose ourselves in the inky river?
Look. I'm at it again, deep in character;
I grip the rail, my heart knocks with knowledge.

Where are you now, Jean-Baptiste Clamence,
with your book-length excuse, your 'confession'?
Too late. Save your words. Stay on the shelf

for I've dropped your plot and find myself entranced
by mine – this will she won't she loop of dying,
this well-worn fiction, like walking on water, or flying.

Diving for Keys

Here we are, bewildered little clowns
    lining up at the deep end

· our trousers socking down
    into the warm overflow.

See how we jump
    one by one

and dropping in fall
    open like Japanese waterflowers

blooming in just these conditions
    of heat, chlorine, piss.

We're stripy, check, burgundy, blue.
    Our hair streams up like roots.

Some hold hands
    even down there.

We all see them, don't we?
    A shimmering loosening silvering out

now very far away on the tiled floor,
    now tentacling up within reach.

No one tries to get them.
    It's enough that they're there;

that we come
    head-butting, panic-motored

back up to the light
    feeling only now

the drag and pull, the full weight
    of our fathers' clothes.

Philosophy for Children

It's time to turn to Nothing, she said, turning
to the board that once must've been black but now
was smeared with years of guesswork and dust.

Where might we find it? Where might Nothing live?
No one spoke. Answer enough, for us.
Tapping her chalk on the desk: Anyone?

She seemed anxious that we know exactly where
to find it, as co-ordinates lead to a *tumulus*
or aeons of digging to earth's burning core.

Death, Space, Eternity
heaved into the airless room
but we saw through them

a bean jar's trinity of light, water, glass
carved in formica a biroed, bleeding heart

Silence held us in its understanding.
Then the bell – a whirl of limbs and intent,
the door swung and swung – then it was still.

Sun

Sole existing witness
to the crucifixion
who saw it all
who warmed the sand
the nails, the pale wood
all the faces looking up
blinking

The Swans

They are the only light
as they come
like a prolonged shock
out of the night
towards us so without
effort I wonder
it isn't the entire inky
lake sliding its way forward.

He coos and chucks from the side
but has no food.
All he wants is for them
to come closer
but who is he to trust?
They hold off,
donate what is theirs
from a certain, temperate distance.

I should never have come.
I want to undo
the idea till it's just that,
refill each glass
till I'm back, straight-backed,
in that oak room
with the last of the sun
and my resolve.

Monogamy

I had a dream
I left you for you.

You said not to do it
and – oh something, I don't know –
had me scrambling back
to home and nestle
in the hollow of your neck.

But you, staring down
at the evening's wreck
of empties and shreds
of black beermat,
said nothing.

I rolled over
and opened my eyes

but it wasn't enough to wake;
my heart lay sunk as a stone

and through the cut and glint of tears
a shoulder reared like land.

You were there
but love, you weren't.

Vigil

'I alone have more memories than all men
have had since the world began.'

           FUNES THE MEMORIOUS, Jorge Luis Borges

All I want is to climb into bed now
with Funes the Memorious
in that back room with the blinds down
and sit there with him, smoking.
We'd stare out in front of us
at the sun-lined window
not saying much and I'd like to

without moving take his hand in mine
(it's soft and pale and a bit bloated)
by which he'd know how in my mind
I feel myself to be only half a soul
like one of those flat fish floating
round half-looking to be whole
again; that till then I just can't seem to –

'Ireneo, my friend' (I'd start like this),
'to say my memory is like a sieve
is to do that utensil an injustice.
What once were pricks are now big black holes
through which every seen, every lived,
every thought thing swoons as if its sole
aim were to forget itself – oh innumerable

things that I can name but not recall!
The first ten bars of *La Gymnopédie*,
the equation for air, the dates of wars,
a leaf, a laugh, a single Aesop's fable,

that good hard quote about grief,
faces round the operating table,
all the stars. All I remember of you

is that you couldn't forget
or stem each prolific detail
(that, and the glow of your cigarette).
So tired you would if you could annihilate
every single shade of every single
green you've ever seen, would wipe the slate
clean of ever seeing green. Ditto blue.

Oh Funes, who dreamt up such strange suffering?
Let us for a moment face each other
and remember something and forget something
imperfectly as others do. Then we can lie
down, calm with our failure, not as lovers
because we know better. Then will you try
and get some sleep? I'll try not to move.'

And as my friend slept I'd remember how
he was going to die in a year's time.
A martyr to the past perhaps he didn't know
when, but I think to him it was all the same;
that by a tear's curve, the slow furring of a lime,
by the blue tint in his stallion's mane,
by his cursed attention to all things, he knew.

Counting

The river's pulled itself away from us.
We count our losses – a dead fox, a shoe.
The sky yields to what we make of it:
mackerel, cirrous, heaven, blue.

We're of this world but still don't know it.
Such busy inventors we're barely here
with all our dreaming, our factory of gods,
our poor old minds at odds with what's there.

No wonder we've failed.
No wonder it's all adding up:
how what we've taken away
will not come back to us

but be returned at a loss:
this gallon can, this slick black wing.
If there was water here we wouldn't see these things;
we'd throw a stone, we'd count the rings.

Matter

And now to this
small matter of you
and me leaning in
to lift you out
of sleep or towels;
this closing in
on what you are:
rich conglomerate
of ligament and blood
and o infinitely
matter of fact
the way you've made
your home here
in this corner
of this house
you dearest happenstance
you *matter of my song*
my small body
of work
of long hours
of small hours
like now when
I lift you up
out of sleep
and into this
good morning
Look! you're here
you real thing
you matter
of life and –

Love! is what
I take from you
this heavensmell
of something leavened
something sweet
something just
about to turn

Cloudwatching

i.m. M. D.

What is it leads the voice
to sing a true note;
what led my hand to take, just once,
yours to cross the street?

Some things we don't need to think:
an embryo settles in the banks of a womb;
a disease, or poem, magicks the first seed
of its irreversible reveal.

Deep inside ourselves but out of our hands
a dream helplessly unfolds
and a cloud seeming not to move
becomes another, so that day

– true to a sense of timing all its own
like lifting our eyes to land on the bird
just landed on that wire
(the one just gone) –

loosed itself upon us:
a rush of blood, the mind shut down
to some quiet default;
your good old heart insisted.

Five days you lay:
your body felled
to a hair's slow push,
the moon rising in a nail.

The Lights

that string out
in front of us,
that lead us on,
that we try to read
and write and love by,
that can't help
but show us the way,
that make us stop and say
We see things now
as we couldn't before ...

We're driving down
a wide street
where always it has
suddenly gone grey
and all the pale heads
lean in slightly
but do not come on
for the lights that string out
in front of us,
that lead us on are dead.

Solace

Then are they glad because they be quiet;
So he bringeth them unto their desired haven
107.30

All morning I've been reading
psalms. I read one then stop

to look out of the window
and now no longer know

if it's the words
or the rain —

a slow steady groundsoaking rain
that's finally come

printing leaves on the paving-stones
putting a shine on things:

the big black bins
the bicycle on its side

the crow and the squirrel
in the steady slow rain

that's filling the buckets
filling the tilt of the green barrow

soaking the cloth
and the old wood bench

that's bashed the fuchsia heads to the ground
and pummelled the weeds in the blacklinered pond

but barely touched
a web the size of my palm

eave-sheltered, trembling
on the other side of the glass

(how delicate the design
and even the odd deviance

but above all
what frailty, what utter disregard!)

– if it's the words
or the rain

that's made me turn
my full attention to

this flimsy shield
this skeletal sun

so that I don't see
either anymore

but hear them fall
silent on stony ground

The Engraver

It has to be a dying art,
this man leaning in with hammer and chisel,
intent on the angle, cut and concision;
all morning on a single word, a name.

His commissioners – each time the same
exacting band of passionate mourners –
want only the best; for this one stone page
to stand for less and more than all their tears.

And as the dates sharpen, the prayer clears
so it all blurs for him; in the end he leaves
what it means to those who already know
just as he leaves the heart of the stone alone

knowing there's nothing there, that deep down
his work is with the surface of things;
the opposite of archaeology
where nothing's found and all is to be made.

The Past

Now is like constantly moving in the centre
of a frame but from this hill looking down
it's stopped and stilled itself into the past:

the path you came by, its dust and stones,
its fellowship of small bright flowers;
this old carved land of field, hedge, wood.

Look, the mind is coming into its own
picture – moving like a hand engraving
a view it might command but never enter.

Some recent poetry from Anvil

MICHAEL ALEXANDER
Old English Riddles

KATERINA ANGHELAKI-ROOKE
The Scattered Papers of Penelope
Edited by Karen Van Dyck

ROS BARBER
Material

NINA CASSIAN
Continuum

TOM DISCH
About the Size of It

MICHAEL HAMBURGER
Circling the Square

JAMES HARPUR
The Dark Age
Boethius: *Fortune's Prisoner*

DAVID HINTON
Mountain Home

GABRIEL LEVIN
The Maltese Dreambook

MATTHEW MEAD
The Autumn-Born in Autumn

DENNIS O'DRISCOLL
Reality Check

RABINDRANATH TAGORE
The Golden Boat
Translated by Joe Winter

PAUL VALÉRY
Charms
Translated by Peter Dale